T0194329

A Walk

with

LIAM

*A Mother's Personal Journey with Her
Special Needs Child from Conception to Adulthood*

Susan Tala Mueller

authorHOUSE®

AuthorHouse™
1663 Liberty Drive
Bloomington, IN 47403
www.authorhouse.com
Phone: 1 (800) 839-8640

Published by AuthorHouse 09/13/2019

ISBN: 978-1-7283-2747-1 (sc)
ISBN: 978-1-7283-2746-4 (e)

Library of Congress Control Number: 2019914177

Print information available on the last page.

Any people depicted in stock imagery provided by Getty Images are models, and such images are being used for illustrative purposes only. Certain stock imagery © Getty Images.

This book is printed on acid-free paper.

This book is dedicated to all the parents of special needs children, who start each day with the determination of bettering their children's lives.

To the soldiers that enlisted in our battle, including the doctors, especially Dr. Suzanne Roberts, and the therapists.

To my dear friends, who lent a shoulder to lean on and open arms to hug, especially Mary Kenney.

To James and Skylar, who sacrificed so much in this journey.

Most of all to Liam, for the lessons he has taught me.

CONTENTS

INTRODUCTION

This book is to serve as a starting point for new parents of special needs children. I share my personal experiences raising a child with disabilities. I do not claim to be a child development specialist, and I do not have a medical doctorate or psychology degree. However, I am a mother who has lived through the despair and triumphs of raising a special needs child. Whether your child was born with disabilities or develops them later in life, the diagnosis can be devastating. My goal is to guide parents through the initial shock. I hope to help them find the necessary strength and direction to help their child—and themselves—live their best possible lives.

The pain is real—but so are the joys. You will lose some friends, and you will gain some new ones. You may discover new interests and new careers. I know many parents who entered the medical field after their child was diagnosed. I became a hyperbaric technologist because of my son. Family members may not understand what you are going through and may distance themselves. Marriages will end in divorce. New, loving relationships will be formed. The disabled child's siblings will rightfully feel that they are not getting equal quality time with you. Your relationship with the other children can be strained, and some of these siblings will go on to have careers in the special needs world. My daughter received her bachelor's degree in social work because of her experiences growing up with her brother.

The road will be bumpy, winding, and filled with potholes. There will be extreme highs, such as when your child successfully completes a surgery, and there will be extreme lows with each new diagnosis or positive lab result. Sometimes it will seem as though no one understands what your day-to-day struggles are. That is okay. In the end, you are not alone. We are an army of parents who wage a daily war against disabilities. We are here. We've got you.

And we are mighty.

CHAPTER 1

ℰᎷℭᎶ

The Journey Begins

"It's positive!" Those were the words that I had been praying to hear for two years. I was pregnant. Once again God had bestowed upon me the miracle of life. The wonderful news came despite what the doctors had told me. I had beaten the odds.

Five years earlier, multiple doctors had somberly said, "Mrs. Mueller, the likelihood of you being able to conceive is very small. Even if you did get pregnant, you would probably not carry the baby to full term. We are recommending a hysterectomy because of the number and size of your uterine tumors. It is the most logical choice."

I let those words sink in: "most logical choice." Maybe it was the most logical choice from their perspective, but it certainly was not from mine. Six months prior to being diagnosed with fibroid tumors, I had met the man of my dreams, who I would spend the rest of my life with. Children were to be a part of that life. A hysterectomy was out of the question as far as we were concerned.

While we were agonizing over our options after my diagnosis, we received a divine intervention. God had made the decision for us. The impossible had happened. I was pregnant with our first child. Skylar arrived during four earthquakes, as a healthy, beautiful baby girl.

After the birth of our first child, I endured two surgeries to remove the tumors, only to have them return bigger and in larger numbers. I endured emergency visits when the tumors would rupture, causing such blood loss and pain that I would pass out. And most agonizingly, I had endured a miscarriage as a result of the tumors.

So, now, here I was at the doctor's office, believing that I had the stomach flu. I couldn't stop vomiting. But it wasn't the stomach flu. It was morning sickness. I was pregnant with our second child. I was elated!

The pregnancy itself was fairly routine. Having been pregnant before, I thought I knew what to expect. But this pregnancy was different. I had minimal symptoms of being pregnant. I rarely had morning sickness after the first few weeks. There was very little edema and no back pain. I was missing all the typical pleasantries that come with the condition. But most concerning to me was the fact that the baby didn't move much. When all my tests continued to be normal, I was told to stop worrying. The amniocentesis had come back normal, and it was a boy. According to an old wives' tale, pregnancy with a male child often has milder symptoms. I accepted that everything was fine. We were happy knowing that our family would be complete with a beautiful daughter and a strong son. We decided that it was time to follow the doctor's recommendation and planned a hysterectomy when our son was born via caesarian section.

The day came for the planned C-section. I had my hair and nails done and was wearing full makeup in anticipation of becoming a mother for the last time. Vanity pregnancy photos had been taken a week earlier, and I posed with a big smile in the hospital, moments before going into surgery. Everything was perfect. Little did we know that everything was far from perfect.

CHAPTER 2

ೱೲ

The Plunge into Darkness

The pictures of me taken before my son was born are difficult for me to look at now. All made up and clowning around in a hospital gown with my big belly sticking out, I had no idea how much our lives would change. From that day forth, there would be no more clowning around. Our lives would forever be overshadowed with the seriousness of having a special needs child.

The beginning of the procedure went as planned. I had spinal anesthesia, so that I could be awake during the C-section. My husband and the doctor were bantering back and forth about the weekend college football game. There was a friendly rivalry between them regarding the teams that were playing. The mood in the room was relaxed and happy.

As our son came into this world, my husband said, "Oh my God, Susan, he is beautiful."

The next words spoken were from the doctor: "He's not breathing."

Everything that followed was a blurry haze. The team rushed our son to another room to work on him. Not knowing if our son was alive, I started to panic. The doctors then fully anesthetized me in order to perform my hysterectomy. As I drifted into unconsciousness, my silent screams could not reach them.

"Stop! I need to stay awake! I need to see my son! I need to know he is alive!" The last thing I remember was tears rolling off my face.

CHAPTER 3

ഇരുഌ

The Jolt into Reality

So many sensations filled me: the sight of the ceiling coming in and out of focus, the squeeze of the blood pressure cuff on my arm, the beeping of the monitor, the sound of the nurse's voice as she urged me back to consciousness. What I didn't sense was my husband holding my hand and smiling at me. Where was he? Nor was there a new, warm baby squirming in my arms, snuggling to get his first meal from me.

From behind my oxygen mask I managed a whisper: "Is he alive?"

The nurse responded, "Honey, I can't tell you that yet. You're in the recovery room. You need to rest. You have been through a lot today. We'll find out about your baby soon enough."

That was not an adequate answer for me. I decided to get out of bed to see for myself. The only problem was that I was paralyzed from the chest down from the anesthesia. I would be for the next twenty-four hours.

As I burst into tears, I tried to get the nurse to grasp the importance of knowing my baby's fate. "You don't understand! I must know if he is alive." I was overwhelmed with grief, knowing that if he did not survive, there would be no more babies for me. I could never try again.

Just then my husband rushed into the room. I barely recognized him. My husband had always been a big bundle of happiness. It is what made me fall in love with him. The ashen-faced man who approached me had eyes swollen red from crying.

"Is he …," I started.

"He is breathing" was all my husband could get out before burrowing his face into my shoulder and sobbing.

While I was under anesthesia, a team of doctors had tried unsuccessfully to intubate my son. Later we would learn that he suffered from a condition called laryngomalacia. The condition makes intubation near impossible without a fiber optic laryngoscope. It would be necessary for every upcoming surgery he would have. The doctors were preparing to do an emergency tracheotomy when our son suddenly started breathing on his own. This was the beginning of many challenges that my son would face and overcome on his own without medical intervention. The ability would earn him the nickname "My Little Warrior."

For the next several hours, I slipped in and out of consciousness. My husband frantically ran between the recovery room and the neonatal intensive care unit (NICU). The next time I awoke, my husband was not there. The nurse stood just outside my door, speaking in low tones with the doctor. She had a concerned expression on her face.

"Doctor," I overheard her say, "it has been several hours, and she still can't even move her toes."

The clock on the wall showed 4:30 p.m. The spinal had been given nine hours ago, and I was still paralyzed. Now new fears washed over me: "How could I take care of my baby if I was paralyzed? How had everything gone so wrong so fast? A few short hours ago I was looking forward to holding my newborn. Now I can't feel anything from my chest down. This cannot be happening. I was told that everything was fine prior to the birth. This was not my first birth. I knew what was supposed to happen, and this was not it."

I had a long, angry conversation with God. "Why God? Why him? Why us?"

He answered me and said, "Why not you? You do not have the blueprint to your life. I do. Be patient. The answers will come. Trust in me." That was the moment I decided to fight.

CHAPTER 4

⍟⍟⍟

The Step Up to Strength

I had to be strong for our new baby. What I didn't know at the time was that the procedure that I had undergone had taken over five hours and included a blood transfusion. Not only did I need to summon up all my mental and spiritual strength, I needed to be physically strong. I wasn't sure if I was up to the challenge, but I knew I had to try. I called for the nurse and demanded that I be allowed to see my baby. She told me that when I was able to move my legs, they would get a wheelchair to transport me to the NICU. I explained to her that that was not going to work for me. She needed to arrange for transport to the NICU on the gurney on which I was lying. And she needed to do it as soon as possible. I would not take no for an answer, and I suggested that she make it happen. Her response was to get the doctor. The doctor gave me the same answer about getting a wheelchair for me, when I was able to sit in one. After a heated discussion, I found myself being wheeled on my gurney to the NCIU.

What I saw when I entered the room took my breath away. In an incubator lay a tiny, ghostly white being with tubes in his nose and throat, distorting his face. He had an intravenous catheter in his scalp and was connected to several monitors. He had pulled out every catheter that they had placed in his arms. His hands and feet looked like little twisted blobs on the ends of sticks. There was not a single hair on his head. There was no movement other than his breathing. But he was breathing.

I started crying all over again. "That is not my baby," I said flatly. "There has been some type of terrible mistake. Take me to my room. That is not my baby." I somehow had this naïve idea that if I could just be with my baby, I could fix everything. I soon came to realize that it would take more than a mother's love to correct this. It would take an army of professionals.

CHAPTER 5

ೞೞೞ

The Quest for Answers

Two words that I became familiar with over the next few years were "rule out." There would be many conditions to be ruled out. But for now, we were thankful that he was alive. In the beginning we were told to consider making final arrangements for our son, as he was not expected to live longer than a few weeks. Those weeks turned into months and then years. He was labeled as a "failure to thrive" baby. Basically, the doctors felt that he would just fade away. They didn't know how determined to live my son was.

We began the hard work of trying to figure out exactly what was wrong with him. Unfortunately, the list of what was wrong with him was much longer than the list of what was right. We were told that he was globally affected. This meant that most of his systems were involved. He was initially diagnosed with microcephaly (small head), hypoplasia of white matter in his brain (undergrowth), CHARGE syndrome, blindness, cleft palate, hydronephrosis (fluid in the kidneys), a heart murmur, pigeon chest (convex sternum), respiratory distress, laryngomalacia, gastric reflux, hearing impairment, scoliosis, congenital vertical tali (both feet were turned backward and the tops of his feet were against the backs of his calves), malformed hands, hypertonia (all muscles were constricted), anemia, jaundice, inguinal hernias, umbilical hernia, cryptorchid (both testicles were retained in his abdomen), and cerebral palsy. There was a possibility that he also had spina bifida. The odds were truly stacked against him. Initially we were overwhelmed with the daunting task of taking on all these health issues. But we had to start somewhere.

My father had taught me that when you are faced with multiple challenges, begin with the most important one that would yield the quickest result. Somehow we had to get nutrients into this little being. Because of his cleft palate, he was unable to nurse. Although he was able to suckle on a special nipple, he would get a few ounces into him and regurgitate them back up. I spent countless sleepless nights pumping breast milk and coaxing it into him. Only minutes later I would be covered in vomit. The doctors suggested that a feeding tube be surgically placed. After much research, I decided to continue trying to feed him without it. And then something miraculous happened. My Little Warrior decided to fight for his life. He began to heal himself.

CHAPTER 6

ঔৎ০৪

The Cavalry to the Rescue

Our first checkup was astounding. A few weeks earlier we had been haunted with the prospect of saying goodbye to our son. Now something amazing and unpredictable was beginning to happen. His condition was improving. His blind cleft palate had closed on its own, allowing him to suckle. There would be no need for a feeding tube. An ultrasound of his kidneys revealed that his hydronephrosis had resolved with no intervention. An echocardiogram showed that his heart murmur had disappeared. The diagnosis of cerebral palsy was ruled out, as was CHARGE syndrome. He did not have spina bifida. Best of all, he was gaining weight.

Medical and surgical intervention was begun in earnest. Medications were given to help with the gastric reflux, and surgeries were scheduled to repair his hernias and cryptorchid. Testing continued to determine what could be done to improve his quality of life. The roller coaster was going up. It would plummet many more times over the years, but for now we were basking in the good news.

Over the course of the first year, Liam was seen by over thirty-five doctors. I would soon quit my job to make it possible to go to all his appointments. There were visits for general pediatrics, ophthalmology, ears nose and throat, audiology, genetics, neurology, orthopedics, pulmonology, cardiology, gastroenterology, endocrinology, radiology, soft tissue surgery, hematology, urology, anesthesiology, laboratory, analgesia specialists, sleep specialists, MRIs, CT scans, occupational therapy, and physical therapy. My home became a revolving door of feeding specialists, vision specialists, nurses, hearing specialists, social workers, special needs equipment vendors, and best of all, well-meaning friends. Suddenly we were surrounded by soldiers that had come to our rescue, with the common goal of helping our son. While it was exhausting, it was also comforting to know that we were not alone in this battle. If our son had chosen to fight, we would support him with all our power. How could we possibly do anything less? We rolled up our sleeves and prepared to go to war.

CHAPTER 7

ഇൗര‌ഗ

The Amble Through Autism

I was beginning to get a handle on Liam's varied diagnoses when I started to notice some subtle changes. He lost the ability to pronounce consonant sounds around the age of two. Prior to that time, he was saying "ba," "ga," "na," "ma," and other typical nonsensical baby blather. Now all he did was scream or stare in silence. He also would not make direct eye contact. It was difficult to get him to smile. We would soon learn why: Liam was autistic.

I distinctly recall the day he was diagnosed. I had taken my daughter with us to the appointment because I couldn't find anyone to watch her. On the ride home, I started to cry. This was alarming for my daughter, as I usually stifled my tears until I was alone. I needed to be strong for her and put on a happy face. As she wiped the tears from my cheek, she asked, "Mommy, why are you crying?" I explained what we had just found out about her brother. "That's okay, Mommy. It just means that he will be able to draw really pretty pictures for us."

My tears immediately turned to laughter. My daughter, not knowing what autistic meant, had thought I said that Liam was "artistic." It would be one of many times throughout my life where Skylar would pull me out of the depths of despair. Somehow, we would deal with this new diagnosis.

Autism would prove to be the most difficult of all of our challenges. With it came a slew of baffling behaviors. Autistic children have many difficulties linked to the disease besides struggling with social interactions.

The severity of their symptoms varies, depending where the child is on the autism spectrum. Children on the high end of the spectrum may be highly skilled in specific areas while challenged in others. These children used to be cruelly labeled as "idiot savants." Autism also used to be called "Cold Mother Syndrome." Some of these kids may be concert pianists but can't have a conversation with someone. Liam is profoundly affected. He is at the low end of the spectrum. He is nonverbal and intellectually delayed. He has gastrointestinal complications, as well as an eating and sleeping disorder. Most distressing of all, he is self-abusive and aggressive with others. Later in life he would develop epilepsy, which I was told is common in autistic males.

We started therapies to help him. Sensory integration sessions were begun, which involved swings and deep pressure therapy. He did tactile therapy that involved immersing him in different textures (buckets of raw beans, warm water, heavy blankets). Feeding therapy was started to try to teach him how to chew and accept textures other than pureed foods. Massage and brush therapy were given to help him accept being touched. Speech therapy began. But the most profound therapy we would discover would be hyperbaric oxygen therapy. It would change our lives forever.

CHAPTER 8

Heaven Sent Hyperbaric Oxygen Therapy

Our family was at a retreat in the mountains, sponsored by an organization for blind children. I was a member of many groups such as this one. It is important to surround yourself with support groups that share information and understand what you are going through. We were having an enjoyable time staying at a cabin in the wilderness. It gave us the opportunity to be together as a family, have some fun, and forget about doctors for a while. They had activities for the typically developing siblings, and Skylar had a blast participating. There were informational seminars for the parents to attend, offering guidance. Most importantly, there were other parents to share experiences with.

I was amazed when I met a young family with twin five-year-old boys who were blind. They were otherwise typically developing boys. Their mother was trying to contain these active little guys, as they were sword fighting with their white seeing-eye canes. She was about as effective as someone trying to herd cats. One of the boys' arms was in a cast. I started a conversation with her after she finally got them under control. She told me that he had broken his arm while climbing a tree in their backyard. Being blind from birth, they didn't realize that they were different than any other active five-year-old boy. I did not envy the challenges that lay ahead for her.

While having a conversation with one of the mothers, we started talking about different therapies that were available. She told me that she had a friend whose son who had severe cerebral palsy and had developed bedsores. He was treated with hyperbaric oxygen therapy for the wounds. As expected, after a few treatments, his wounds began healing rapidly. Everyone was astounded when for the first time in his life he smiled and said, "Momma."

I sat in disbelief. Could this be the miracle we were praying for with Liam? I had to find out.

When we got home, I searched the internet for hours about hyperbaric oxygen therapy. I learned that there were many applications for hyperbaric oxygen therapy. Some indications were approved and covered by insurance, but many were not. None of Liam's conditions were covered by insurance. We would need to find a way to pay for the treatments ourselves.

I started a fundraiser at a community center to help cover the cost. Each treatment was two hundred and fifty dollars. They were scheduled in blocks of forty consecutive treatments. While people were very generous, I began to realize that it would take a long time to accumulate enough for the treatments. I am not a patient person. I wanted to get started now. We decided to put a second mortgage on our house.

Friends and family began to question my sanity. I ended a friendship over my actions. The friend could not understand why I was doing this and called me foolish and reckless. How could I get us so deep in debt on an unproven therapy? I had done my research, and the potential for a positive outcome far outweighed the negative side effects from the therapy. The most common side effect was barotrauma to the ear drums from the inability to equalize. Liam had already undergone a myringotomy and had tubes in his ears. This would not be a complication.

The deciding factor for me was when I meet a woman named Carol Leon. Carol and her husband Sam were the owners/operators of Hyperbaric Healing Center. More importantly, she was the mother of three special needs kids who had benefitted from hyperbaric therapy. It had also saved her life at a time when conventional doctors had told her to make final arrangements. From the second I meet her; I knew I could trust her.

Liam had a list of ailments that we hoped hyperbaric therapy would help. One of Liam's diagnoses was cortical blindness. His eyes moved independently from each other and constantly fluttered. He could not stand on his own, let alone walk. He didn't crawl either. He would scoot on his bottom to get places. He was not sleeping more than a few hours at a time. Getting him to eat was nearly impossible. He suffered from chronic constipation and chronic pain. And of course, there was the autism.

We started the treatments when Liam was almost three. He took well to them and often fell asleep while in the chamber. The effects were immediate. After his first treatment, he slept ten hours straight. Concerned, I got up at one point during the night to make sure he was still breathing. He was sleeping blissfully, like any typical baby. The next morning he was ravenous. He ate all his breakfast without any hesitation. He had a large normal bowel movement and seemed comfortable.

We continued the treatments for six days a week, with one day off. The treatments would continue for several months. After the third treatment, he started tracking. His eyes moved purposefully in unison. After one of his treatments, I was standing next to him with his bottle in my hand. He looked up at me from his stroller, took the bottle from my hand, and started drinking it! Not only could he could see, but he could hold the bottle himself!

The progress he made from that point was astounding. He slept at least eight hours every night. He had a normal bowel movement daily. Mealtime turned from a source of frustration to a source of pleasure as his appetite increased each day and he learned to feed himself. He was able to stand and eventually would learn to use a walker after thirty treatments. The most significant improvement was that he started to become engaged in the world around him. Videos and toys became fun activities for him. A smile returned to his face and mine.

The reaction amongst his doctors went from skepticism to astonishment. I remember a conversation with one of his doctors when I was seeking her opinion on hyperbaric therapy, prior to starting. She told me that it was unproven, a waste of money, and a builder of false hope to parents. Her advice was to find an institution and walk away. "After all," she said, "you have one healthy child to concentrate on. He will always be exactly as you see him today." I left and never went back. I wish I could have seen her reaction to him after hyperbaric therapy, but thankfully, she retired soon after our visit.

We went to the ophthalmologist for a recheck after our first set of forty treatments. This was the same doctor who six months earlier had diagnosed Liam with cortical blindness. He had advised me at that time that there were no treatments, surgeries, or corrective lenses to resolve the condition. The doctor walked into the room with a sad look on his face, not expecting to see any improvement. Liam sat on my lap as the doctor rolled toward us on a stool. Imagine the shocked expression on his face when Liam reached out, grabbed his tie, and began tracing the teddy bears on it with his other hand.

"He can see! What have you been doing? How is this possible?" he exclaimed. I told him he had been receiving hyperbaric treatments. He was so impressed that he wrote a letter of recommendation, declaring how hyperbarics had improved Liam's vision.

Hyperbaric therapy is an adjunct therapy. It is intended to be used in addition to other support therapies. We like to use the analogy that hyperbaric therapy fills the gas tank and turns on the ignition. Other therapies combine to help drive the car.

Everyone involved with Liam was amazed at his progress. He began responding to his physical therapy and was able to climb stairs alone. He also mastered how to ride a tricycle. To this day, riding his bike is one of his favorite activities. I liked to say that I was a witness to miracles on a daily basis.

Hyperbaric therapy became a passion and soon a career for me. I went to school, passed the national board exam, and began working at Hyperbaric Healing Center as a Certified Hyperbaric Oxygen Technologist. Carol was kind enough to give me an employee discount for Liam's treatments. Over the years, Liam would receive over two hundred treatments, with improvements noted after each block. And then we reached a plateau, where no significant improvements were seen. For a child that was never supposed to see, hear, or walk, his progress was amazing. I am grateful for the advancements we made with hyperbaric therapy.

Carol and I coauthored an article that was published in an autism magazine. I am thankful to Carol and Sam for everything that they did for Liam and my family. We remain friends to this day.

Later I went to work at a multi-chamber facility at the university to increase my knowledge of hyperbaric therapy. I returned to school to receive my Certified Hyperbaric Oxygen Technology-Veterinary certificate, allowing me to work with equine, dogs, cats, and even rabbits. Working with animals has also been my passion. I have worked in the veterinary field for most of my life. It was a logical choice to combine the two. I have seen both humans and animals benefit from hyperbaric oxygen therapy. To the medical professionals who doubt hyperbaric oxygen therapy as a viable alternative, I say the proof is in the results.

CHAPTER 9

The Stumble to Slumberland

Liam was never a good sleeper. The only time he slept through the night was when he was receiving hyperbaric treatments. He would nap for an hour or so throughout a period of twenty-four hours. It was rare for him to sleep longer than four hours at once.

Liam had several overnight sleep studies done through the years. They were all inconclusive. It was possible that he had sleep apnea, but the doctors could not say with certainty. His EEG showed some abnormal brain wave activity, but it was difficult to decipher if this was the cause of his insomnia. They thought that his circadian rhythms were off but weren't sure why. In the end, no one knew why he couldn't sleep.

Not having a cause, we decided to treat the symptom. Over the years he was started on multiple medications, with varying results. We began with the most benign drug: melatonin. Melatonin is popular because of its effectiveness for most people. Liam is not one of those people. We have tried it at many stages of his life, and it doesn't work. When he was two years old, he was on a double adult dose. He may as well have been taking sugar cubes because he did not sleep. We tried again when he was a teenager, and we think it gave him night terrors. My daughter says that it gives her bad dreams. He would fall asleep and wake up an hour later, screaming and banging his head on the wall. Melatonin is not our friend.

We tried diphenhydramine. We didn't know at the time, but Liam has a paradoxical reaction to diphenhydramine. Instead of sleeping, he would jump up and down in his bed for hours. That was not a good time. We discovered that this is not an uncommon side effect.

And then came the big guns: "Let's try lorazepam," the doctors said. "It will relax him enough to fall asleep." Again, Liam had a paradoxical effect, causing him to hallucinate. He stared at his hands and screamed in terror for hours. That was not fun either.

Liam's physical therapist suggested that we try sensory integration therapy at night. We installed a swing from his ceiling. I cannot tell you how many hours I pushed that swing while he giggled in delight. He was happy, but he still wasn't sleeping. We also did massage therapy to try to put him in a drowsy state—nothing. We gave him warm bubble baths before bed. While he enjoyed them, he did not sleep.

Summer came, and we went to a pool party at our friend's house. Liam paddled around with his little floaties on, grinning from ear to ear. He jumped up and down and squealed with exhilaration. Afterward, he would sleep! Liam's favorite holiday is now the Fourth of July. He gets to go swimming before we go to the fireworks display. He gets so excited watching the night sky light up; I need to remind him to breathe. And then we go home and sleep. It has become my favorite holiday as well.

But every day can't be the Fourth of July. Since Liam is nonverbal, it has always been a detective game to try to figure out what is bothering him. Is he in pain? Where does he hurt? Is he constipated? Eyes bleary, I would plead with him through what felt like endless nights: "Why don't you sleep?"

I finally accepted that this was our life. I used to joke that I would sleep when I was dead. Until then, I would endure Liam not sleeping at night.

Many autistic children have sleep disorders. When they are up all night, they develop fun little games. Some of Liam's favorite games are turning on and off lights, ceiling fans, and faucets. He also enjoys opening and closing drawers, the dishwasher, and doors. All my outside doors are double-locked at night, so that he won't escape. The most dangerous habit he has is running through the house and pounding his head on the wall. His aggression is not only self-directed. Most nights he wakes me up with a punch to the stomach, followed by a fistful of my hair being pulled. I sleep with one eye open. Of course, all these fun activities are accompanied by bloodcurdling screams. I am surprised that the neighbors have never called children services on me. I am certain it sounds as though someone is being murdered.

Recently we entered the fascinating world of psychiatry. We received a whole new gamut of drugs aimed to control the aggressive behavior and help Liam sleep. We started with zolpidem, with minimal effect. We increased his night dosage of his seizure medication with no change. We went on to risperidone, which caused him to drool so excessively that he would choke on his own saliva. Quetiapine was started, which caused his feet and hands to develop painful edema.

Look out, Liam—here comes paroxetine! Liam received one dose of paroxetine and was sent into a psychotic crisis. He was sweating profusely and extremely agitated. I had to put him in four-point restraints to prevent him from injuring himself or me. The nurse had gone home for the day, and the doctor was closed. My only option was the emergency room, and I wasn't prepared to go there yet. I decided to ride it out with him and monitor him for any life-threatening signs. If they developed, we would go to the ER. I took his vitals repeatedly over the next hours as I mopped the sweat off his forehead. His blood pressure, temperature, and respiratory rate were all within normal limits. His heart rate was slightly elevated but still within normal limits. Eventually the storm passed, and we both fell asleep exhausted.

I called the doctor the next morning to tell him about the horrendous night we had endured. His response was, "Frankly, I have tried most available options. Our next step is to prescribe lithium." Wait, what? Isn't lithium prescribed for schizophrenia? Liam had not been diagnosed with schizophrenia. I politely declined his offer.

I decided to try to go with a holistic approach. We started on a combination of GABA, L-5-hydroxytryptophan, and low-dose melatonin. It worked for a few weeks, and then it stopped working. We switched to doxylamine succinate which had a paradoxical effect. We were up all night. We tried chamomile and rose hips, with no effect. We tried a combination of bromelain, valerian root, hops extract, and lavender, with no effect. We even tried liquid cannabis. The results were all the same: Liam did not sleep.

I decided to change Liam's environment. I added a special weighted blanket to his bed to provide pressure therapy. A memory foam topper was added to his mattress. I installed a special light that had soothing sounds and projected a simulation of waves from the ocean onto the ceiling. I think Liam was chuckling at these attempts. They were not effective.

I was at Liam's school one day and started talking with one of the other moms about sleep issues. She told me that she had started her son on L-theanine. L-theanine is an amino acid that promotes relaxation and increases focus. The results were immediate. He was no longer self-abusive, he smiled more, and he slept. Everyone who worked with him at school noticed the change, as did his psychiatrist. Unfortunately, like most medications with Liam, the effects were short lived. Soon he was aggressive and not sleeping.

For now, we have gone back to a lower dose of quetiapine, to avoid having his feet and hands swell. Some nights it works; most nights it doesn't. I would like to say that we found the magic elixir that induces sleep for these children, but that will be someone else's discovery. For now, I still sleep with one eye open.

CHAPTER 10

❧

The Problem with Parents

It has been my experience that most special needs parents—present company included—are a little, how to put this politely, off. The constant struggles to get services that our child needs and deserves, the extreme highs and lows of their medical conditions, and the sleep deprivation can make a person question their sanity. It changes the hard wiring in our brains. Over the years I have befriended many parents that, if I hadn't had Liam, I may have avoided. We can spot each other in a crowd.

The grocery store can be a terrifying place of sensory overload for a child with autism. The bright lights, loud overhead speakers, and masses of people can turn what is a mundane task for most people into a nightmare for special needs moms and dads. Yes, we special needs parents see each other. We nod knowingly and send a smile of encouragement as the child hits the floor in a tantrum. There always seems to be that one person that doesn't understand what is happening. Suggestions of a good butt whooping or other forms of corporal punishment are usually given by these folks.

"My child would never be allowed to act like that," they say smugly as the scurry by. Good for you! You have a typically developing child with you, and I don't. Go spank your own kid but leave mine alone.

I used to carry business cards in my wallet that said "My child has autism. Please be patient." On the bottom was information suggesting they educate themselves about autism. I would hand them out in the grocery store, until I ran out of my first box. I gave up when I realized that these people preferred to remain ignorant.

Liam and I were shopping in a home improvement store once. He had recently had his leg casts changed, and they came up to his knees. He was sitting in the cart and had figured out how to kick his casts on the metal part of the cart. There was a woman shopping next to us, with an angry expression on her face. She was annoyed by my child seeking sensory input by kicking the cart. I hardly noticed it. Suddenly, she came over and hissed at him as she placed her hands over his casts to get him to stop. I grabbed her hands and in a blind fit of rage threatened to break her fingers if she didn't let go. She turned pale and backed away. We continued shopping, as if nothing had happened. You can mess with my mind, you can mess with my money, but don't mess with my kid. Yep, we special needs moms are crazy.

People will say the silliest things. One time we were at the grocery store, and Liam had his hearing aids on. Normally I would take them off before we went in, but I was in a hurry and forgot. A woman walked up to our cart and put her face an inch away from his.

At the top of her lungs she yelled, "Those are the cutest little hearing aids I've ever seen!" Liam jerked away from her, wild eyed, and started screaming. She said, "Oh, I'm so sorry. I didn't mean to scare him."

"Really?" I said. "Well you did; now go away."

I came to expect these types of interactions with people that don't understand disabled children. What is more frustrating to me are the parents of special needs kids that are floating up the river of denial.

Liam used to attend a school for autistic children. Some students had multiple disabilities and were more severely affected than Liam. The school would have group therapy sessions for parents once a month. I attended two meetings as an observer. I listened to the other parents and didn't provide any input. By the third meeting, I was becoming increasingly weary of their stories of sunshine, rainbows, and butterflies. They sounded as though life was peaceful and perfect. Gosh, wasn't it great to be a special needs parent? They smiled and cooed as they talked about changing poopy diapers at 3:00 a.m. on a kid that weighed eighty pounds and was trying to take their head off in the process. There are labors of obligation, and there are labors of love. The previous was not a labor of love.

Finally, I couldn't take anymore. When it was my turn, I stood up and said, "I'm sorry, but I thought that we were in a safe haven that allowed us to share the challenges of being parents of special needs children. Don't get me wrong; I love my son. But this is my third meeting, and I am beginning to feel that I am the only one that does not enjoy all the daily struggles that we sustain. I don't find any humor in getting punched by my son at 2:00 a.m. I would love to know what it is like to sleep more than four hours a night. And no, I don't look forward to changing poopy diapers." I looked at the mom who had told the story and noticed her eyes were welling up in tears. "Can we all get real here and agree that our lives are much more difficult than the parents of typically developing children? It is the life we have been given, and we all make the best of it. But please stop suggesting that every minute of every day is a joyous event to be envied by other parents." All at once, everyone stood up and applauded me. The poopy diaper mom burst into tears and came over and hugged me. I hugged her back. We are all in this together. Let's not try to make out like this is the life we would have chosen for our children or ourselves.

Three of my favorite T-shirts say, "You can't scare me, my kid has autism," "It is what it is," and "Don't worry, I've got this." That pretty much sums up my life. This is not the life I wanted, but I will make the absolute best of it.

CHAPTER 11

ఇంచిత్

The Fragility of Friendships

Friendships have always come easily to me. Being an extrovert makes me approachable to most people. My brother once told me that he envied my ability to comfortably enter any social situation. He used the analogy of a cat being dropped: no matter what environment I was put in, I always landed on my feet. The ability to talk with anyone anywhere about anything is second nature to me. But keeping friendships requires more effort. This became most evident after Liam was born.

When I was pregnant with Liam, we moved to a rural area. My neighbor had a daughter Skylar's age and a one-year-old boy. Our connection was immediate. We began a friendship that would develop such a strong bond over the years that we felt more like sisters than friends. We shared secrets about our lives that we had not told anyone else. Skylar stayed with her when I delivered Liam. She would become a lifeline for me after Liam was born. There would be times when she came to my house, took one look at my exhausted, tear-stained face, and rescued me. Countless times she would walk into my home and take Liam from my weary arms. "Give him to me," she would say. "Go over to my house and crawl in bed for a while." I would hand Liam to her as he was screaming and flailing. As I walked across the street for some much-needed rest, I would hear him stop crying. She was born to be a mom, as she had the uncanny ability to calm him down. She would pull me from the depths of despair many times over the course of our friendship. Because of her sense of humor, she could always make me laugh, when all I wanted to do was run away from home. Our daughters became best friends as well. They would play with dolls for hours on end. Her son was a sidekick to the girls' fun.

The blinders that I had placed on my head prevented me from seeing anything but Liam's needs. Our friendship, like all my relationships, began to erode. It became lopsided. I became a taker, and she was the giver. I didn't have the time, energy, or interest to listen to what was happening in her life. My life was more dramatic and important than hers in my opinion. Like all sisters, we started having fights. She would call me a martyr. She accused me of being self-centered and uncaring about anyone other than Liam. I called her a whiner. She had a loving husband, two healthy children, and a beautiful home. What could she possibly have to complain about? Her life was perfect; mine was a disaster. I didn't want to hear about it, and I told her so.

We went from talking every day to not speaking for weeks after these fights. I turned a deaf ear to her attempts to try to reconcile. I was much too busy taking care of Liam to concern myself with her feelings. Like everything and everyone in my life at that time, she didn't matter. Nothing mattered except Liam.

Although she has since moved, we have remained friends. However, our relationship has been tainted by my inability to acknowledge her life struggles. There is no such thing as a perfect life. We all have our difficulties. Being a special needs mom does not give someone the license to be calloused to what others are going through. Sisters we are no longer. We are more like second cousins who only see each other at weddings and funerals. I think of her often, and it saddens me to know I forfeited such a special friendship because of my all-consuming mission to put Liam above everyone else.

I began a friendship with another woman almost twenty years before Liam was born. I was her maid of honor twice; she was mine when James and I got married. We were there for each other when our children were born. She got pregnant at the same time I became pregnant with Liam. We talked daily on the phone about the impending births. Wouldn't it be funny if one of us had a girl and the other a boy and they fell in love? We would laugh at all the scenarios of our two children growing up together.

One day her husband called to say that she was in the hospital. She had suffered a miscarriage. When I went to see her, I was ashamed of my big belly as she lay in her bed, pale from blood loss, and weakly smiled at me. None of us knew it at the time, but this would be her last pregnancy. There would not be more babies for her.

After Liam was born, she came to visit me at my home. I did not allow any visitors at the hospital except my husband. When I changed his diaper, his legs were constricted against his chest because of his hypertonia. "My babies always struggled like that when I changed them," she said casually. I stared at her in disbelief. She made some other comments that showed she had no idea of the seriousness of Liam's condition.

After I started a fundraiser for Liam's hyperbaric treatments at a community center, I went to her house to tell her about the progress. I was bewildered when she started shaming me for doing the fundraiser. "How dare you ask people to donate money to you when your husband has a full-time job? You don't even know if this treatment will work. And now you are going to put a second mortgage on your house? I think you are foolish!" she yelled at me. Obviously, she had no idea of the magnitude of my endeavor. The fact was, she didn't understand the whole special needs experience I was going through. I didn't have the time or energy to explain it to her. I walked out of her house, slamming the door behind me. It would be the last time we ever spoke.

We have a friend of the family that we affectionately call "Aunty." She worked with James when I met him, and we instantly became friends. I have yet to meet a person as beautiful on the inside and outside as she is. We used to throw elaborate Halloween parties, and she was the head of the decorating committee. Arts and crafts are her thing, and she is very talented. Skylar has spent hours doing crafts with Aunty. At Christmas time we would make ornaments for the tree. Hers were always the most elegant. For a while she owned a home a few blocks from us, and we would see each other almost daily. Liam enjoyed her company, as she was gentle and kind to him. She would babysit for us when I couldn't find a nurse for Liam. This allowed James and me to go out on a date. When we asked her to be Liam's godmother, she didn't hesitate.

Even though she was engaged once, she has yet to marry. Whether she is very selective, or men are blind to the treasure that she truly is, she remains single. She will make a great mom someday. Being the kind soul that she is, when her parents became ill, she left her life here and moved into their home out of state to care for them. About once a year she returns to visit friends and family. I look forward to her visits. I wish we talked more often, but when we do, it is like she never left.

After I joined a pool league, I became friends with a girl that had a Janis Joplin vibe. She was a free spirit who could not be bothered with the opinions of others. We would shoot pool together and enjoyed a friendly competition. She was a good player, and I learned some new skills from her. As our friendship developed, we started spending more time at each other's homes. Her home was decorated in shabby chic and was charming. When I complimented her on the design, she told me that she had decorated it herself. Not having much fashion sense, I asked her to help me. We spent days painting walls, reupholstering chairs, and updating the backyard décor. It was fun and therapeutic. When I first met her, she prided herself on being independent. There was no need for a man in her life, she would tell me. That was until she met a man that swept her off her feet in a whirlwind romance. After a short time, he encouraged her to move in with him. Her world was turned upside down to accommodate him. Her cute little house was rented out, and most of her belongings went into storage. After a few months of living together, he became bored and asked her to move out. She was devastated.

After they broke up, she was inconsolable. Every time I saw her, she would sob and complain about how cruel he was. I was on my own teeter-totter relationship with my husband at the time. I soon grew tired of listening to her, and I told her so. I was in the process of ending a relationship of twenty-five years, and they had been together less than a year. Suck it up, sister. Again, my problems were so much more important than anyone else's. I told her that if she couldn't stop talking about him when we were together, then we couldn't hang out anymore. Of course, her pain was as real as mine. I just didn't want to hear about it anymore. Eventually I stopped taking her phone calls. We haven't spoken in a long time, and I feel guilty for being such a crappy friend.

Another example of a friendship failure is between my mother-in-law and me. She was a strong, opinionated woman, and we were good friends from the moment we met. I grew to love her and called her "my other mother". Everywhere she went, she was the life of the party. She was well liked by everyone she met. She was a "tell it like it is" kind of person and never shied away from voicing her opinion. Most times I admired her for that. The time that I didn't would become the end of our relationship.

We went on a family vacation, and my mother-in-law came with us. We didn't bring a nurse with us. By the time the trip was over, I was exhausted from taking care of Liam. On the long drive home, we stopped at a crowded restaurant. As we sat down, I felt a sense of dread come over me. Liam could not handle loud, crowded places, and I anticipated a meltdown. Everything was fine until we were halfway through our meal. He became overloaded and lost it. He started screaming and pounding his head with his fists. As I stood up to remove him from the situation, my mother-in-law said something I would never forget: "Don't you think your life would be easier if Liam wasn't here?" It is important to note that she did not say, "Don't you wish he was dead?" or "Don't you wish he had never been born?" But that is what I believed she was insinuating. My response was immediate and filled with anger.

"How dare you say that about your own grandchild?" I shouted at her as I stormed out of the restaurant, causing a scene. The remainder of the ride home was extremely uncomfortable. She kept trying to apologize and explain her remark. I was not having it and yelled at her to shut up. For years she continued to try to repair our relationship. She was met with cold silence from me.

Looking back, I realized why her comment upset me so profoundly. That same thought had crossed my mind, but I was too stubborn to admit it. Of course our lives would have been easier without Liam. But he was here, he was my son, and I loved him. It was my obligation to protect him. Those were the facts. My martyr syndrome had been in full defense mode. The next time I spoke with her was on her death bed. She passed away the day before her birthday, which, ironically, was also my birthday. From the hospital, James held the phone to her ear as I sang "Happy Birthday" to her. She was gone twenty minutes later. I take solitude in feeling that we made our peace before she left. I wasted so many years being angry at her in my manic attempt to protect Liam. I miss her quick wit and laugh. Rest in peace, you sassy lady.

Some of my friendships are over twenty-five years old. Many of them are long distance friendships. I have a friend I met while we were working together as animal technicians. When we are together, we both laugh so hard that my face hurts and I almost wet myself. We don't share the same political beliefs, and we don't always agree on how the universe works. However, she has the biggest heart of anyone I have ever met, and I love her to death.

After hurricanes devastated the Gulf Coast region, she persuaded me to accompany her to help with animal rescue. She had volunteered for disaster relief before, so she knew what to expect. We were stationed at a high-ground shelter for the animals being transported out of the eye of the storm. The shelter, which served as a makeshift MASH unit, was packed with one thousand dogs and one thousand cats. Every morning my friend and I would part ways. I would go work with the dogs, and she would attend to the cats. We were there for a week, working ten-hour days. Exhausted, each day we left the rescue covered in pet food, cat litter, and varying forms of animal excrement. We would wash the day off and share a glass of wine as we prepared to do it all over again the next day. It was a life-changing experience that I am proud to have been a part of. Thank you, my friend, for including me in that adventure. Let me know where to meet you when the next disaster strikes.

One of my dearest friends is someone I met in junior high school. We have been there for each other through marriages, divorces, births, and deaths. She is a highly intelligent woman, who is financially savvy. Raising four children on her own has forced her to be this way. She works hard, and now, because of circumstances beyond her control, she is faced with the daunting task of raising several of her grandchildren. We often compare notes on whose life is more difficult. I say she wins; she says I win. In reality, it's a tie. We each struggle in our own way.

We can go for months without having a conversation and pick right back up where we left off. I have traveled to visit her at her home, and she has come to see me. We have met in vacation spots on a couple of occasions and had a great time. This year we have two trips planned. The first one coincides with our forty-fifth high school reunion. (I know—we are old.) We are taking a few days to stay at a resort. The second trip is a seven-day cruise for my birthday. We have each planned for our households to be taken care of in our absence. Hopefully our homes will still be standing when we get back. I can't think of anyone more deserving to go on these trips with me. She gives so much to her family every day. It will be nice to recharge our batteries together. Don't forget your corkscrew for the cruise, my friend. I can hardly wait for the adventures to begin.

While going through this journey with Liam, I have met many, what I call, transitional friends. These are special needs parents who are going through the same struggles I am. We develop a bond with each other. We share the intensity of the situation we are experiencing, exchange phone numbers, promise to stay in touch, and then never hear from each other again. It is not sad; it is just a fact. In our busy lives we lose track of people. It happens.

Each of my friendships serves a purpose. Some friends are there to listen, and some are there for me to listen to. Some are there to lend a hand when it is most needed, or vice versa. Some are there to receive advice from me, and others are there to teach me. My friends are varied in their backgrounds, beliefs, and occupations. The thing that all of them have in common is that we make each other laugh. I love each of them deeply. My mother used to say that if you can count your close friends on one hand, you are lucky. I am fortunate to call you my friends, and I cherish each one of you.

CHAPTER 12

8008

The Revolving Door of In-Home Care

No one will ever be able to provide the quality of care that you as a parent can give to your child. Let's face it. At the end of the day, our child is not their child. From the beginning we knew that we needed help. Over the years I have gone through many nursing agencies and even more nurses. I treat my nursing staff like family. We share dinners with our nurses. They have gone on vacations with us. A few of them have remained friends with us long after they stopped working for us. They will witness the good, bad, and ugly of your day-to-day life. While you will do your best to keep your homelife private, the nurses are immersed in it. Every heartbreak, every victory, every struggle, and every argument will be seen by them. People say that you can't chose your family—this is the one exception.

I didn't know what to expect when we got our first in-home nurse. We were fortunate to get an experienced licensed vocational nurses (LVN) who was working on becoming a registered nurse (RN). She had three children of her own, and Liam became as much of a part of her family as she was of ours. Sometimes she would bring her youngest child to work with her. The baby was not much older than Liam, and they would parallel play together. There were a few occasions, after she had been with us for years, that Liam would spend the night at her house. She would take him after I had endured too many sleepless nights in a row, so that I could get some rest. None of this was allowed by the nursing agency. If they had found out about our arrangement, she would have lost her job and I would have been dropped as a client. I am not suggesting that you follow my example. Sometimes you need to do what works for your family, and this worked for us. It is a reality.

She was authorized to attend school with Liam, and I will be forever thankful for that. Seeing Liam go off to kindergarten was stressful for me. It was comforting to know that she would be my ears and eyes while he was there. She developed a friendship with the teacher that lasted long after she stopped working for us. Eventually she became pregnant again and had to leave us. I still miss her to this day.

After she left, the nursing agency began sending nurses with varying levels of incompetency. The first nurse arrived in an old Volkswagen beetle that sputtered, smoked, and died in front of my house. She appeared to be around seventy years old, with long, stringy gray hair pulled back with a peace sign bandana. At the time Liam was eating jarred baby food. When she didn't have the strength to remove the lid from the jar, she started to cry.

"Please don't tell the agency that I can't do my job here," she said, tears streaming down her cheeks. "I desperately need this job." My heart broke for her as I placed my hand on her shoulder and led her to the door.

The next failed attempt came in the form of a quiet, middle-aged woman. When new nurses come to us, I will stay with them for several shifts, showing them how I like things done. I will then watch them for a few more shifts. Eventually I will leave the house to do short errands. Everything seemed fine for the first two stages of training with this particular nurse, so I decided to go the grocery store. It was evening and dark outside. I had not been gone more than fifteen minutes. When I returned, I walked into Liam's room and noticed that the lights had been turned off and the room was dark. He was watching a movie, and the nurse was rocking back and forth in his rocking chair with her arms crossed tightly against her chest. Shocked, I asked her what she was doing.

She continued rocking frantically as she replied, "I should have told you that I have bi-polar disorder and am prone to fits of rage. When I get upset, I turn the lights off and hug myself." What the actual hell! I could not even speak as I escorted her out of my house and locked the door behind me. The following day I advised the nursing agency that they needed to improve their screening process.

The next disaster was a gentleman from a foreign country. After my previous experience, I decided to stay with him for many shifts. When he had been with us for about two weeks, I offered to make dinner for him and asked what his favorite dish was. I was about to learn how to make moussaka. Being a pretty good cook, I felt I was up for the challenge. I had never eaten moussaka and was not sure what it should taste like. It turned out awful. I called it "moussucka" because it sucked. We choked it down, and he told me that it was the worst meal he had ever had. "Fair enough," I thought. "I hated it too."

He proceeded to tell me how fortunate we were to live in America. He said, "In my country, children like your son would be left at the hospital to die. They have no worth." I didn't know if that was true about his country or his personal belief. Either way, I told him, "Here's your hat. There's the door. You can leave now."

Sometimes nurses arrive that are a good fit for you, but you are not a fit for them. That was the case with the next nurse. She was an attractive, young, bubbly LVN that was studying to get her RN. She was very competent, and Liam tolerated her well. My daughter was in awe of her because she was "so cool." She stayed with us for a short while, until she passed her RN test. She then went on to a more challenging job. We enjoyed having her work with Liam and our family.

Many of the nurses have taught me specific skills. A fiery, middle-aged woman started working with us while Liam was still eating jarred baby food. "I want you to taste this," she said to me during one of her first shifts. I took a bite of the baby food and almost spit it out. It was bland with a slimy texture. "Would you eat this?" she asked me. "I don't think Liam should be made to eat this either. From now on we will make homemade stew and puree it for him. I will teach you how." We got a big pot and filled it with chicken broth, chicken, carrots, celery, onions, garlic, zucchini, yellow squash, potatoes, sweet potatoes, cumin, salt, pepper, basil, bay leaves, and oregano. After about an hour, we strained everything and put it through the food processor. What came out was delicious! Liam ate pureed food for the rest of his life. I still make stew for him in big batches and put some in the freezer. After a few years with us, she moved to be with her adult children. She may be gone, but her cooking lessons have stayed with me.

Liam had a nurse that treated him like his own son. They would go swimming at the community center together. He took Liam to the park. He treated Liam like a typically developing child. He was not afraid to let him get down and dirty, something that I cringed at. Liam could act like a rough and tumble guy when he was with this nurse. We trusted that he would be safe in his care. The nurse was also an excellent caregiver and attended to Liam's every need. When Liam first started having seizures, he was the one that noticed the subtle facial twitching. These twitches would later lead to grand mal seizures. He went on numerous family outings and vacations with us. Every evening we had family dinner together. Medical issues ended his employment with us. When he went for surgery, we sadly said goodbye. He and James have remained friends and will occasionally hang out together. He is a great nurse as well as a friend.

Liam has chased away a few nurses as a result of his aggressive behavior. One of these nurses was a quiet, polite woman who worked seven days a week elsewhere. She did one shift a week at our home. She also filled in shifts if my regular nurses were sick or on vacation. She was with us for many years until Liam became too strong and aggressive for her. I don't fault her for leaving, and she was a great help while she was with us.

The next nurse that Liam ran off was a big, strong guy with twenty years' experience working with autistic children. He worked with us for a month. One day I went out to run some errands. He called me in the middle of his shift to tell me I needed to come home right away because he was leaving and would not be back. Liam had proven to be too much for him.

Our current nurse has been with us for over five years. She has three children of her own who have sacrificed spending time with their mother because she is here with us. Liam does not get away with his tantrums with her. We have an expression at our house: "There is a difference between autism and bratism. You just need to know what the signs are." She is excellent at determining if Liam is having a meltdown because of his autism or if he is being a brat. As she says, "I'm not having it," she will redirect him to stop the tantrum. Liam respects her, and so do I. Even though she and Liam are the same height, she is not intimidated by him. Whatever task needs to be completed, she calmly works through him losing it until the job is done. Haircuts, nail trimming, brushing teeth, shaving, administering medications, feeding and other things that trigger Liam into a fit get accomplished during her shift. She is hardworking, patient, and kind while taking care of him. It is not an easy task, but she handles it with grace. We are fortunate to have her here and hope that she will stay for a long time.

All my nurses have taught me lessons. The bad ones taught me the warning signs when someone should be a former employee. The good ones have taught me that there are special skills required to work with disabled children. They have treated my son with dignity, respect, patience, and compassion. They have given me the confidence that he would be okay in the care of a stranger. He can be difficult to work with. I appreciate them being here, allowing me to take a break.

If you are reading this, you know who you are. I owe a debt of gratitude to these special chosen members of my family.

CHAPTER 13

80C3

The Trudge into the Teenage Years

Becoming a teenager is difficult even for a typically developing child. For the special needs child, it can be almost unbearable. I remember lots of eye rolling, door slamming, and sassy remarks from my daughter. She once said to me, "I hate you! You don't understand what I am going through! No one does!" This was followed by the slamming of her bedroom door. I let her cry it out, and an hour later she gave me a big hug and told me that she loved me. You've got to love those hormones!

For disabled children, puberty can be very challenging. I can only imagine what it is like to have a special needs daughter begin menstruating. It was hard enough to have a typically developing daughter go through that. For Liam the addition of testosterone increased his aggressive behavior. He would pound his head with his fists and bite his fingers until they bled. His tactile defensiveness increased to where he no longer tolerated his glasses or hearing aids. We went through many pairs, as he would become agitated, rip them off, and stomp them on the ground. We eventually gave up. He also developed epilepsy around this time. Autistic boys will often start having seizures once they enter puberty. Liam was no exception.

The teenage years are also a time when our children start having feelings toward the opposite sex. My daughter had always been attractive, and the boys really started to notice her. Thankfully, she was never too boy

37

crazy because she was an athlete. She prioritized playing water polo over playing the field. It has served her well over the years.

Liam attended a special school for autistic children. Skylar and I went to prom with Liam, as his dates. He loves to dance, or at least his version of dancing, which mainly involves jumping up and down. I came to realize that this is the most popular dance move amongst the autistic crowd. The dance floor was filled with students jumping up and down. Most of them were nonverbal teenagers bouncing around, flapping their arms in the air, grunting, and screaming. To an outsider I am sure it was a confusing picture. As the mom of an autistic child, it filled my heart with joy to see all of them having so much fun.

Liam had caught the eye of a pretty, shy girl. He and I were on the dance floor when she came running up to us several times, arms flapping, squealing in delight. Because Liam lives in a parallel universe to most of the world, he just ignored her. She was persistent. She would run up next to him, giggling, and then dart back to her seat. It was very sweet to witness.

We had some snacks, danced for a while, and then Liam had a meltdown. Like many of the kids there, he had reached sensory overload. Some of the students wore sound blocking headsets to lessen the stimulation of the music. The loud music and bright lights combined with the crowd of people became overwhelming for Liam. It was time to go. I would fondly remember the prom as a day when Liam came as close to being a "normal" teenager as he ever would. It gave me such happiness to see him find pleasure in this rite of passage.

CHAPTER 14

ℰ𝒰ℭ𝓑

The Missteps to Treatments

One of the most important lessons I learned early in our journey is to trust your own instincts. As a parent you know your child better than anyone else. I took the information I was given by trained professionals and weighed it with my own mother's logic. You need to be an advocate for your child because no one is as qualified as you are. I am not suggesting that I know more than a doctor about my son's condition. But I do know my son, and I know what makes sense. I have done therapies, such as hyperbarics, that I was told were a waste of time. I have refused procedures and medications because I knew my son's history better than a new doctor. It is possible that they didn't read my son's entire chart before prescribing a medication or procedure that was contraindicated for his condition. It is possible that they were not experienced with a case as complex as my son's. Regardless, never be afraid to question a doctor on a decision they have made. They are making educated guesses based on their wealth of knowledge. That is why it is called "practicing" medicine.

My son was scheduled to have a very complicated surgery to repair his twisted legs. The anesthesiologist came to me to discuss his role in the surgery. When I told him that they would need a special device called a fiber optic laryngoscope, he condescendingly chuckled at me. "I have been doing this for many years. I think I know better than you what your son requires," he said to me.

My response was, "I am certain that you are very familiar with all forms and procedures of anesthesia, but I know my son. No disrespect intended, but he will require a fiber optic laryngoscope. Please make certain there is one available in the surgery suite." The doctor flashed an all-knowing smirk at me and said he would make sure it was there.

After the seven-hour surgery, the doctor approached me with a newfound respect, saying, "Good call. We had to use the fiber optic scope to intubate him. Thanks for the heads-up."

After his leg surgery, Liam had casts on both legs, up to his hips. There were three pins in each foot. He had one entering each big toe and exiting his heel, with two additional pins crossed at his ankles. The doctors had rotated each foot one hundred and eighty degrees. A new artery had been built in each leg. He was started on morphine intravenously for the excruciating pain. I sat by his bed, watching his monitors, as I do every time he is hospitalized. As I gazed at his face, I noticed that he was becoming pale. His pulse oximeter rapidly dropped from 90 percent to 75 percent. This meant that his oxygen concentrations were falling. He was going into respiratory arrest! I hit the nurse button and ran into the hall, yelling for help. The crash team rushed into the room to frantically begin CPR on Liam. I heard over the speaker system, "Code blue, room 309"—Liam's room.

The next thing I knew, there were two security guards restraining me, preventing me from re-entering the room. I was hysterical as I fought to regain entry.

From out of nowhere came a booming voice, "Sit down now!" It was one of the mothers that I had befriended in the surgery waiting room, while our children's surgeries were being performed. She took me by the shoulders and physically placed me in a chair outside Liam's room. She was a slight woman, but at that moment she had the strength of a sumo wrestler. "How do you think you can help your son? You will only get in the way of the crash team," she said. "Let them do their job." Of course she was right. I could only watch from the hallway when my son began screaming as they reversed the morphine with naloxone. The pain flooded his body, but he was breathing again. The team stabilized him, and he was transferred to a private room.

What followed is an example of trusting your mother's intuition. While waiting to talk to the doctor, I had to physically restrain Liam as he writhed in pain. As I held him, I saw a very young doctor peek into the room, my son's chart in his hand.

"Mrs. Mueller," he said, "I am one of the interns on your son's case. He received an overdose of morphine, causing respiratory arrest. I am going to start him on some acetaminophen for the pain."

Standing there, smiling at me, he seemed very pleased with his decision. But his facial expression soon changed to bewilderment when I responded to him.

"Tell me doctor," I said. "Are you going to make a paste with the acetaminophen and rub it on his casts? Or are you planning on giving it orally? My son just endured a seven-hour orthopedic surgery. He has three pins in each foot, and you are going to stand there and tell me that the only analgesics in this hospital are morphine or acetaminophen? Please go get the senior doctor and the pain management team. You are dismissed!"

Was it rude and mean of me to say those things? Absolutely. But when it comes to my son, I am not running for Miss Congeniality. My purpose is to obtain the highest quality care possible for him. If someone's ego gets bruised or feelings get hurt, that is none of my concern. I can assure you that the intern learned something that day and will remember me. You are welcome, Doctor.

During another hospital stay, an intern also learned the value of prescribing the proper medication. Liam had emergency surgery on his elbow joint. He had developed methicillin-resistant Staphylococcus aureus (MRSA) from a scrape he got from a fall on the driveway. While at the hospital, he developed pneumonia with MRSA in his lungs. Because MRSA is a bacterial infection, which is resistant to many antibiotics, he was started on three powerful intravenous antibiotics that gave him horrible projectile diarrhea. One of the interns decided to start him on rectal acetaminophen suppositories to manage his pain.

Morning rounds included the parents. The team came to our room, and after the senior doctor had presented Liam's case, she asked if I had any questions.

"Yes," I said. "Which doctor here prescribed rectal acetaminophen for my son?" A young man raised his hand. "Could you please explain your logic for giving any rectal medication to a child that has watery, projectile diarrhea?"

The senior then spoke up and said that she would also like to hear the reasoning behind his decision. The team looked at him for an answer, the young man mumbling something and slinking to the back of the crowd. Again, I was happy to assist in continuing his education.

I have always considered my son's best interest when making decisions for him. Whether it is medical, educational, or financial decisions, I always think of what is most beneficial for him. I have successfully sued the school district three times for denial of services and improper placement. I have stood up against many government agencies, insurance companies, and doctors over the years. I have always made my son my number one priority. I am not saying this to make myself out to be some type of hero. These are examples of how much strength is required to get what your child needs and deserves. I have won some very important battles over the years. But in the process, I lost many things that were just as important as my son's rights. Most notable, I lost myself.

CHAPTER 15

ഔയങ

The Precarious Path of Relationships

Before Liam was born, I prided myself on my appearance. After he was born, I paid no attention to anything but Liam. I quit my job. I stopped going to the gym. My diet consisted of whatever fast food was available on the way to the doctor's office. My overeating was justified in my mind because I was stressed. Since my family members have a tendency toward being overweight, it was only a matter of time before I gained seventy pounds. Cutting and coloring my hair took too much time and effort. I stopped going to the hairdresser. The same was true for getting manicures and pedicures. Shopping for clothes was out of the question because that money could be spent on Liam. My makeup bag was collecting dust in the closet because it wasn't used anymore.

I was not the only one being neglected for the sake of Liam. My daughter was suffering as well. My life was engulfed with caring for Liam. When we weren't at appointments or in the hospital, I was on my computer, relentlessly researching new treatment options. All other aspects of my life became secondary.

My daughter often said to me in anger, "It's always all about Liam! What about me?"

My response was, "How could you be so selfish? You're smart, healthy, and beautiful. He needs me more than you do." I could not have been more wrong.

My theory is that typically developing siblings of special needs children have two options: They get lost in the shuffle, or they become overachievers. A child can end up craving attention so much that they act out. This can be in the form of doing poorly in school, associating with the wrong crowd, drinking, or doing drugs and other illegal activities. If the parent does not pay attention to these signs, it can lead to depression, anxiety, jail time, or worse.

The alternative route for the "normal" child is to become an overachiever. This is what my daughter chose. Skylar has always been very critical of herself. She never felt smart enough, pretty enough, thin enough, or good enough. Nothing could be further from the truth, and I blame myself for this. She once told me, when I congratulated her on an excellent report card, that it was her responsibility to do the best she possibly could at everything. She told me, "I have to be extra good to make up for my brother"—what a terrible burden for a child to carry through life.

Over the years there would be missed birthday parties, Thanksgivings, water polo games, slumber parties, field trips, and many other important events in Skylar's life. Liam was hospitalized on an average of ten days every year until he turned nineteen. He could not be left alone at the hospital. It was my duty to stay by his side.

One of his hospital stays coincided with Skylar moving into the dorms at her college. For the first time ever, I called one of his at-home nurses and paid them to stay with him so that I could go with her to move in. I knew that the ward nurses at the hospital would be too busy to monitor him properly. He needed constant supervision, as he would pull out his IV catheters.

While I worried if Liam would be okay, I couldn't be in two places at once. This time Skylar would be the priority. I am so glad that I made that choice. We had a great weekend together as a family. I was filled with pride as my daughter set out on her first steps to independence.

As James and I drove back home, I could feel apprehension build in me. The hospital, with Liam lying helpless in a bed, loomed in front of me. I went directly there from dropping my daughter off. What special hell would await me was anyone's guess.

When I got to the hospital, Liam was alone in his room. The nurse that I had hired left when his shift was over. I had gotten stuck in traffic returning from Skylar's college and was two hours late. Liam was screaming in pain and covered in diarrhea. Snap—back to reality. I called for the nurses to help me clean him up and get some pain medication on board. As I had a reputation for being difficult, they were quick to respond to my request. After he was dozing off in a drug-induced sleep, I cleaned myself up, poured myself a coffee, and settled down to have another conversation with God. Quietly I prayed, "Dear God, will this ever end?"

Unfortunately, his response was, "I am sorry, my child. I can't give you the answer to that." I dozed off in the chair to await another day.

My relationship with my daughter improved as she matured. She began to realize that I had done the best I could. In her sophomore year of college, she told me that she was pursuing a degree in social work. American Sign Language was her chosen foreign language, and she was becoming fluent in it. Her interest was not with the special needs child or even with the parents. She wanted to work with the siblings of special needs kids.

"Mom," she explained, "who will be better at understanding the struggles they go through than me? I have lived it every day of my life." I was so proud, and relieved, to know that I hadn't been such an awful mom after all.

During this time my husband and I had our own struggles. I had let myself go to the point where I was unrecognizable. I was fat and out of shape. My long gray hair was past my elbows and always secured in a ponytail so that Liam could not pull it. My wardrobe consisted of my husband's old, faded work T-shirts and either baggy sweatpants or baggy jeans. The dark, puffy circles under my eyes could not be hidden by makeup, even if I knew where to find it. I had given up on myself. All that mattered was Liam.

We were rarely intimate. We didn't hold hands or hug each other. I give James a lot of credit. He never gave up. He would plan weekend getaways that I would cancel because I couldn't schedule a nurse. He made dinner reservations that I would not go to because it might conflict with the nursing schedule.

And then James got sick. He developed a chronic cough that was initially diagnosed as tuberculosis. He was hospitalized for the first time in his life, and he was scared. A bronchoscopy was performed, which revealed that he had Valley fever. This condition is caused by inhaling microscopic organisms from the soil. James worked in construction, and it was believed that he had contracted it on the job.

I had become so accustomed to hospitals that I treated this episode as an inconvenience and not much more. After all, Liam had undergone bronchoscopies, along with many other procedures. I had grown numb to getting too worked up about medical procedures. James was a grown man. He could handle this. It was no big deal—except that it was. This would be a turning point in our relationship. James needed me, and I wasn't there for him.

Once James was released from the hospital, he began treatments that improved his condition. He continued to try to get close to me. I was in my own world, and there was no room, or time, for anything other than taking care of Liam. James tried to be affectionate with me, and I would tell him to stop pawing me.

I distinctly recall an episode where once again he was vying for my affection. I was sleep deprived, as always, and lost my patience with him. I screamed at him, "Why can't you just leave me alone! You are suffocating me! Why don't you go get a girlfriend and let me do my job?"

So that is what he did. I found out about the affair the weekend before Valentine's Day. My car got better gas mileage, and we had exchanged vehicles so that he could take my car to Skylar's distant water polo game. I saw a Valentine's card in the side pocket of his truck. "How nice," I thought, "he got me a card." But this card was not for me. And it wasn't the only card there. Included with the blank Valentine's card was a dozen love letters from another woman. I will not go into details, since it is too painful, but let's just say they were very adult in their content.

I laid the cards on the table, and when James came home, I demanded an explanation. In a knee-jerk reaction, I filed for divorce the next day. I accept full responsibility for my part in the erosion of our marriage. You can only ignore and reject someone for so long before they will seek attention elsewhere. James would tell me later, in one of our many therapy sessions, that he sought someone else after his stay in the hospital. He felt I had made it clear that I didn't care about him. I made him feel dead inside. He needed to feel alive again, and she did that for him.

We suffered through many therapy sessions filled with arguments, tears, and attempted reconciliations. What had happened here? How had we let our lives spin so far out of control? How could I have treated the only man I ever loved so cruelly? How could he betray me? Was there a way back from this?

I didn't have the answers, but I knew that something had to give. It had to start with me. It was time for some serious introspection and change.

I started by cutting off twelve inches of my witchipoo hair and donating it. I dyed it blonde. I joined a gym again and went every day. I became a pescatarian, and I cut out all fast food. I got a new job operating a hyperbaric chamber at a veterinary office. I joined a pool league to meet new people. Within six months, I had lost seventy-five pounds. Was any of this going to change my marriage? I wasn't sure, and honestly that was not my goal. I needed to love myself again before James, or anyone else, could.

James and I have remained friends. We acknowledge the role each of us played in destroying our marriage. Someone once advised me to choose wisely and treat kindly. If you don't do the first, you can't do the second. We had chosen each other wisely, but we certainly had not treated each other kindly. We will always love each other deeply. Do we still have a future together? It is highly unlikely, considering that our divorce is final—but only time will tell. After all, we are both still alive.

CHAPTER 16

◕◓

The Road to Independence

"There is a mass in the cerebellum," the doctor said.

"Well, that is interesting," I thought. But the diagnosis wasn't Liam's this time. It was mine. I had begun having some strange and alarming episodes. They would begin with my face flushing and my heart pounding. The symptoms would progress to include nausea and vomiting, slurred and stuttering speech, uncontrolled muscle movements, blurred vison, and the sound of glass bottles clanging in my ears.

The first episode resulted in an ambulance ride and overnight hospitalization. The tests were begun. Bloodwork and radiographs were taken. I had a brain CT scan, echocardiogram, ECG, and MRI. The results were inconclusive. I was kept overnight for observation. In the morning my symptoms had resolved, and I was released.

The next episode was a carbon copy of the first one. This time Skylar, who is an EMT, took my vitals and drove me to the emergency room. Again, all the tests were normal. The emergency room doctor suggested that I was having a panic attack. If he knew me, he would have known that my current life was stress-free when compared with my previous life. Sitting at my bedside, my daughter rejected that idea. She insisted there was something medically wrong with me. This was not a panic attack. He referred me to a neurologist who studied the test results and concluded that there was something abnormal in my cerebellum. The neurologist was concerned that I might also have tumors in my gastrointestinal tract that were causing problems.

An appointment was scheduled with a gastroenterologist for an upper and lower GI study. When those results came back normal, he ordered a urine test to rule out endocrine-secreting carcinoid tumors. Sounds scary, right? The test came back negative. I was then sent to an ear, nose, and throat doctor, who ordered a complete audiology examination to rule out any problems there. No significant findings were reported. I had an ultrasound of my carotid arteries to check for calcium blockage. It came back normal for my age. The EEG was normal as well.

While these tests were being performed, I developed some new symptoms. I became confused at times. One morning I put Liam's medication in my coffee instead of creamer. I caught myself before I drank it. I attempted to take the trash out to the mailbox and stood there bewildered as to why I would do that. The oven had me completely perplexed one day as I tried unsuccessfully for thirty minutes to turn it on. I would forget to turn the burners off on the stove once my food was cooked. The most alarming result of my confusion was when I overdosed Liam with his night medications. We had another ambulance ride to the emergency room. They flushed the drugs out of his system, and he was kept overnight for observation. Fortunately, he was okay.

I developed ataxia. I wasn't dizzy. I just couldn't figure out how to place one foot in front of the other. It resulted in two falls in the shower. I noticed that the ataxia worsened after exercising or taking my dog for a walk. Stress also made it worse. I discovered this while taking Liam to his annual neurology appointment. These appointments are always stressful, but that day he was more aggressive than usual. He had broken the arm restraints on his wheelchair. When I bent over to repair them, he hit me in the face. I lost my balance and fell into a chair. After the appointment, I gathered Liam up and proceeded to go home. I could not have predicted what happened next.

The following day I received a call from the social worker for the neurology department. They had filed a complaint with adult protective services. I began to feel panic rise in me. Did they honestly think that I was abusing my son? Ironically, the complaint was against Liam for elderly abuse. The tables had turned. Now I was being perceived as the one that needed help. She explained that they were required to report any acts of abuse that they witnessed.

The social worker for adult protective services came to my home to interview me. I had a short-sleeved shirt on. When she saw the defensive bruises on my arms, she asked me if I was afraid of living in my house with Liam. The thought had never crossed my mind. Of course I wasn't afraid of my son. He had gotten bigger and stronger; I had gotten older and slower. I wasn't as quick to dodge his outbursts anymore. It was as simple as that. She filed her report and told me that she would be recommending that appropriate housing be found for Liam. Given my current medical condition, I reluctantly agreed.

I went back to my neurologist, who was perplexed as to what my diagnosis could be.

"Hey, Doc, how about I have a lump in my brain?" I inquired. He said that he had not seen a mass this small, in this location, cause so many problems. This was above his level of expertise, and he was referring me to neurology at the university. I am still waiting for my appointment.

As for Liam, I knew that eventually I would need to find proper placement for him. I will be sixty-three years old this year, when he turns twenty-one. While I still have a lot of spunk left, I realize that I am not immortal. I would rather choose a home for him now than have him placed by a stranger after I am gone.

The process has begun for Liam to live away from me. I will continue to fight for him to get the best possible care. Mixed emotions fill my heart daily.

I have done everything humanly possible to improve Liam's quality of life. Many sacrifices have been made on this journey. In the end, would I choose to do it again? It was never an option. He is my son. Whether he loves me or not, I will never know. He has never hugged me, kissed me, or told me that he loves me. None of that really matters. I have enough love for both of us. May God guide you, My Little Warrior, as you continue your journey on the road of life. Take comfort in knowing that Mommy will always be watching over you.

FINAL NOTE

If you take nothing more than the following from this story, I will have done my job. You will be sleep deprived and confused by the barrage of information you receive. My ex-husband started a journal for our son to help with this. The cover page had all his personal and medical information (name, address, phone number, parents' names, birth weight and length, blood type, allergies, medical record number, insurance information, and social security number). Following the cover page was a list in column form of doctor appointments with doctor's name, specialty, date and time of appointment, reason for visit, and distance to appointment (for tax purposes). The middle portion of the book contained what happened at each appointment, beginning with the doctor's name, date, and vitals, including height and weight.

I am in the medical field, so I did this in the form of a SOAP: subjective (chief complaint), objective (results from physical examinations and tests), assessment (diagnosis), and plan of action. The final section of the book contained all contacts names, phone numbers, and addresses. The book served as a guide to where we had been and what the next step was. I call it Liam's bible, as his complete medical story is in there. It has saved me many times from the confusion of dealing with multiple doctors and agencies. You will have several of these journals over the years, and I keep them in chronological order by year. The doctors have told me that I am a great historian for our son, but I really did it for my sanity.

SAMPLE JOURNAL

Cover page

Name

Address

Phone #   Date of birth

Father's name   Mother's name

Birth weight/height Blood type

Allergies

Insurance co.   Policy #   Group #

Med. record #   SSN

Appointment section of journal

Date/time of appt.	Dr. Name/specialty	Reason for visit	Miles
10/20/2017 10:00 am	Dr. Jones/neuro.	Initial consult	47
11/16/2017 8:00 am	Dr. Smith/GI	Swallow study	47
12/01/2017 11:00 am	Dr. Joe/ortho.	Cast change	38
01/20/2018 2:00 pm	Dr. Jim/soft tissue	Test results	32

Middle section of journal (description of visit)

Date: 01/20/18 Height/weight: 5'2", 100 lbs. Temp: 98.6°F BP: 120/60 Heart rate: 80 bpm

Dr. Name/specialty: Dr. Jim/soft tissue surgeon

Reason for visit: Test results

Physical exam/test results: There are incomplete closures of the abdominal wall on the left and right sides of the inguinal area, as well as umbilical area. Testicles are not present in the scrotum.

MRI results: Incomplete closure of abdominal wall in left inguinal area, 1 cm by 2 cm, right inguinal area, 1.5 cm by 2 cm, and umbilical area, 2 cm by 2 cm. Both testicles are retained in the abdominal cavity, 3 cm distal to the transverse colon.

Diagnosis: Bilateral inguinal hernias, umbilical hernia, cryptorchid

Plan: Surgery to repair all hernias and properly place testicles in scrotum. Consult surgery scheduling for appointment. Contact anesthesiology for presurgical consult. Submit presurgical bloodwork and urinalysis.

Back section of journal

Name/specialty or agency	Phone number	Address
Dr. Jones/neuro.	(323) 555-1234	123 S. 1st Anytown, USA 00000
Dr. Smith/GI	(323) 555-4321	123 S. 1st Anytown, USA 00000
Dr. Joe/ortho.	(323) 555-3456	321 N. 2nd Anytown, USA 00000
Dr. Jim/soft tissue	(323) 555-6543	456 W. 3rd Anytown, USA 00000

REFERENCE WEBSITES

This is a partial list of the most common afflictions with which our children are faced.

Autism

Asperger/Autism Network	aane.org/aha-landing-page/
Autism Asperger's Sensory Digest	autismdigest.com
Autism Society	autism-society.org
Autism Speaks	autimspeaks.org
National Autism Association	nationalautismassociation.org

Blindness/vision impairment

American Council of the Blind	acb.org
American Foundation for the Blind	afb.org
Braille Institute	brailleinstitute.org
Guide Dogs of America	guidedogsofamerica.org
Guide Dogs for the Blind	guidedogs.com
National Eye Institute	nei.nih.gov
National Federation of the Blind	nfb.org

Cancer

Alliance for Childhood Cancer	allianceforchildhoodcancer.org
American Childhood Cancer Organization	acco.org
Children's Cancer Research Fund	childrenscancer.org
Coalition Against Childhood Cancer	cac2.org
Stand Up To Cancer	standuptocancer.org
St. Jude	stjude.org

Cerebral Palsy

American Academy for Cerebral Palsy and Developmental Medicine	aacpdm.org
Cerebral Palsy Foundation	yourcpf.org
Easter Seals Disability Services	wecelebrate.org
United Cerebral Palsy	ucp.org
United Cerebral Palsy Alliance	ucpa.org

Deafness and hard of hearing

Alexander Graham Bell Association for the Deaf and Hard of Hearing	agbell.org
American Academy of Audiology	audiology.org
American Cochlear Implant Alliance	acialliance.org
American Society for Deaf Children	deafchildren.org
National Association for the Deaf	nad.org

Developmental delays

Center for Parent Information and Resources	parentcenterhub.org
Parent to Parent USA	p2pusa.org
Center on Technology and Disability	ctdinstitute.org
Individuals with Disabilities Education Act	sites.ed.gov/idea/

Down syndrome (trisomy 21)

Global Down Syndrome Foundation	globaldownsyndrome.org
National Down Syndrome Congress	ndsccenter.org
National Down Syndrome Society	ndss.org
United Parent Support for Down Syndrome	upsfordowns.org

Diabetes

American Diabetes Foundation	diabetes.org
Diabetes Research Institute Foundation: Parents Empowering Parents	diabetesresearch.org/PEP-Squad
Juvenile Diabetes Research Foundation	jdrf.org

Epilepsy

Epilepsy Foundation	epilepsy.com
Epilepsy and Services Support	dailystrength.org/group/epilepsy-seizures
MyEpilepsyTeam	myepilepsyteam.com
Epilepsy Support and Education Services, Inc.	epilepsysupportnm.org

Gastroenterology and hepatology disorders

American Liver Foundation — liverfoundation.org

American Gastroenterology Association — gastro.org

Celiac Disease and Gluten Free Support — celiac.com

Crohn's Disease and Colitis Foundation of America — ccfa.org

Hyperbaric oxygen therapy

International Hyperbarics Association — ihausa.org

National Board of Diving and Hyperbaric Medical Technology — nbdhmt.org

Undersea and Hyperbaric Medicine Society — uhms.org

Nephrology and urology disease

American Kidney Fund — kidneyfund.org

Kidney and Urology Foundation of America, Inc. — kidneyurology.org

Renal Support Network — RSNhope.org

National Kidney Foundation — kidney.org

Orthopedic impairments

United Spinal Association — unitedspinal.org

Orthopaedic Institute for Children — ortho-institute.org

National Center on Physical Activity and Disability — ncpad.org

Shriner's Hospitals for Children — shrinershospitalforchildren.org

Spina Bifida Association — spinabifidaassociation.org

Pulmonary and lung disease

American Lung Association — lung.org

American Thoracic Society — thoracic.org

Cystic Fibrosis Foundation — cff.org

Pulmonary Fibrosis Foundation — pulmonaryfibrosis.org

Additional services

Contact the department in your state for further information.

Advocacy (national)

Council of Parent Attorneys and Advocates, Inc. — copaa.org

Special Needs Alliance   specialneedsalliance.org

Government agencies

Social Security Administration   ssa.gov

State agencies

Department of Developmental Services: Regional Center Location List   dds.ca.gov/RC/RClist.cfm
Department of Health Care Services: California Children's Services   dhcs.ca.gov/services/ccs
Medi-Cal   medi-cal.ca.gov
Medicare   medicare.gov
Department of Social Services   cdss.ca.gov

This list is compiled by best overall ranking. Each hospital is followed by specialty ranking.

Top ten children's hospitals

1. **Boston Children's Hospital** (cardiology #2, diabetes and endocrinology #2, gastroenterology #2, neonatology #3, nephrology #1, neurology #1, orthopedics #1, pulmonology #4, urology #3)
2. **Cincinnati Children's Hospital Medical Center** (cancer #1, cardiology #8, diabetes and endocrinology #3, gastroenterology #1, neonatology #5, nephrology #2, neurology #2, orthopedics #4, pulmonology #3, urology #2)
3. **Children's Hospital of Philadelphia** (cancer #2, diabetes and endocrinology #1, gastroenterology #3, neonatology # 2, nephrology #4, neurology #6, orthopedics #2, pulmonology #2, urology #1)
4. **Texas Children's Hospital** (cancer # 6, cardiology #1, diabetes and endocrinology #6, gastroenterology #4, nephrology #3, neurology #3, pulmonology #1, urology #4)
5. **Children's National, Washington D.C.** (cancer #7, diabetes and endocrinology #10, neonatology #1, nephrology #6, neurology #5, orthopedics #8, pulmonology #9)
6. **Children's Hospital Los Angeles** (cancer #9, cardiology #5, diabetes and endocrinology #5, gastroenterology #5, neurology #9, orthopedics #5)
7. **Nationwide Children's Hospital** (cancer #5, neurology #7, orthopedics # 9, pulmonology #6, urology #10)

8. **Johns Hopkins Children's Center** (cancer #10, nephrology #10, neurology #4, orthopedics #10, urology #7)
9. **Children's Hospital Colorado** (cancer #8, diabetes and endocrinology #7, gastroenterology #7, neonatology #4, pulmonology #7)
10. **Ann and Robert H. Lurie Children's Hospital of Chicago** (cardiology #3, gastroenterology #8, urology #5)

Additional hospitals ranked by number of specialties (not included in top ten overall)

Seattle Children's Hospital (diabetes and endocrinology #4, nephrology #8, neurology #10, urology #8)

UPMC Children's Hospital of Pittsburgh (cardiology #6, diabetes and endocrinology #4, gastroenterology #9, pulmonology # 8)

St. Louis Children's Hospital (neonatology #9, neurology #8, pulmonology #5)

Monroe Carell Jr. Children's Hospital at Vanderbilt (pulmonology #10, urology #6)

Children's Medical Center Dallas (cardiology #7, gastroenterology #6)

C.S. Mott Children's Hospital (cardiology #4, neonatology)

Children's Healthcare of Atlanta (gastroenterology #10, nephrology #7)

Dana-Farber/Boston Children's Cancer and Blood Disorders Center (cancer #3)

St. Jude Children's Research Hospital (cancer #4)

Phoenix Children's Hospital (cardiology #9)

Le Bonheur Children's Hospital (cardiology #10)

Yale New Haven Children's Hospital (diabetes and endocrinology #8)

Rainbow Babies and Children's Hospital (neonatology #6)

UCSF Benioff Children's Hospital San Francisco and Oakland (neonatology #7)

New York-Presbyterian Morgan Stanley Children's Hospital (neonatology #8)

Children's Mercy Kansas City (nephrology #5)

Lucile Packard Children's Hospital Stanford (nephrology #9)

Texas Scottish Rite Hospital for Children (orthopedics #3)

Nemours Alfred I. duPont Hospital for Children (orthopedics #6)

Rady Children's Hospital (orthopedics #7)

Riley Hospital for Children at Indiana University Health (urology #9)

Printed in the United States
By Bookmasters